Predictions for 2013-2014

Kurt B. Bakley

authorHOUSE®

AuthorHouse™
1663 Liberty Drive
Bloomington, IN 47403
www.authorhouse.com
Phone: 1-800-839-8640

First published by AuthorHouse 11/11/2011

ISBN: 978-1-4670-9421-4 (sc)
ISBN: 978-1-4670-9420-7 (e)

Printed in the United States of America

Dedication: In memory of Lon Bakley

Contents

Introduction   ix
Chapter One   Coded earthquakes   1
Chapter two   Other predictions for 2013-2014   7
Chapter Three The Carving   13
Chapter Four   The Trumpets and Sun   15
Chapter Five   The end   18
Chapter Six   Come to Christ   22
Chapter Seven The Codes   32
About the Author: 69

INTRODUCTION

In this book I will show how coded messages in the Bible, Nostradamus and ancient Egypt art predicted two earthquakes for 2013 and 2014. I also will show other predicted events using those sources for the year 2014. Chapter seven in this book shows how and where I get these codes for the predictions of 2013-2014.

The predictions made in this book are sometimes based on Chinese astrology. In Chinese astrology there are 12 signs that rule one year every 12 years. Unlike our astrology that rules one month every year. The cycle of every 12 years means that predictions can be based on those yearly cycles. In another words the year 2014 minus cycles of 12 years backwards can tell us what will happen in 2014. Ecclesiastes 1:9 states that things that now happen happened in the past the same as the ancient Egyptians and Mayans believed. If 1906 is the Chinese Year of the Horse and 12 year cycles brings it to 2014, and is again the Chinese Year of the Horse, than things that happened in 1906, like the great San Francisco earthquake, could happen again in 2014.

Another difference of Chinese astrology is that it rules two hour time periods each day. Since there are 12 signs this covers a 24 hour time periods of a day that each sign rules. The signs in our astrology don't do that. And in Chinese astrology the 12 signs also rule our 12 signs and 12 months. The polar opposites of these signs, Chinese, or ours, are connected to the same date, time and event. If an event in May-June (Gemini) of 2014 is predicted, then in November-December (Sagittarius) of 2014, the polar opposite is when the same event may happen. The great San Francisco and/or Seattle earthquake and possible tidal waves could strike again in May- June, or November-December of 2014, the Chinese Year of the Horse, which rules Gemini that rules San Francisco and Seattle. See cities ruled by signs in Chapter seven: *The Codes* for this information. As I just said the great San Francisco earthquake of 1906 was the Chinese Year of the Horse the same as 2014. This also holds true for the great earthquake that hit Los Angeles in 1857 is the Chinese Year of the Snake the same as 2013. The Chinese Snake rules our Taurus sign and month of May. The city of Los Angeles is in the Taurus zone as told in chapter seven and is ruled by Leo. The Leo sign (lion) runs from July 21-23 to August 21-23 and with its cusp of seven goes to August 28-30. Does the term "Babylon the great is fallen, is fallen," in the book of Revelation 18:2 mean two times Los Angeles is hit by an earthquake? Are those two earthquakes the one on January 17, 1994 that hit Northridge and the other "one hour" away as Revelation 18:17 predicts? Change the hours to one day of 24 hours and then change to years added to 1994 and it equals 2018-2019 when the second earthquake happens in Los Angeles. See Revelation chapter 6. The earthquakes of 2013 and 2014 might be in other places of the U.S. and world. Or is Babylon, a spiritual name for the U.S. and especially Los Angeles, fallen twice that of 2013 or 2014 and then again in 2018-2019 right when the sun goes into a supernova and causes the earth to shake and be utterly destroyed like Revelation 6:12-17 predicted? The "one hour" Babylon the great is fallen, is fallen that Revelation 18:2-3,6,10 predicts in one hour, or 60 minutes, changed to six years added to 2013, counting each year or not, equals the years 2018-2019. The "wine of the wrath of her fornication" in (verse 3) when these quakes and wrath happens, could mean the wine harvest, which is August-September or possibly June-September of 2013, 2014 and 2018-2019. Those months are in the fourth (June-July), fifth (July-August) or seventh month (September-October) of the Bible's calendar as Zechariah 7:3,5, 8:19 predicts.

If these prophecies fail for those times given in this book then other dates of July-August of 2013-2014 and 2018-2019 may come true for that event or the other events.

Chinese astrology begins it New Year of the certain sign on the second new moon after the winter solstice. This means New Years Day is different each year and begins sometime in January or February each year.

I also use in this book year/chapter codes of the Bible told of in Chapter 7: *The Codes.* This is where a chapter in the Bible means a certain modern day year plus or minus the Chinese 12 year cycle.

If this book fascinates you then be sure to read my next book *Predictions for 2015.* Also read *About the Author* at the end of this book for all my other books you may want to read. It tells you where you can buy them because they are only available at a web site given. It will also tell you which ones to read first and how to read them, which is very important.

August 29, 2011

Kurt B. Bakley

Chapter One

Coded earthquakes

Over the years I have noticed a pattern in earthquake (and tidal waves?) predictions. There is a code that can sometimes predict earthquakes. It doesn't happen all the time, but every once an awhile it does. The code is based on Song of Solomon 6:10 "banners" and the Greek word for commotion or earthquakes and the words near them, which are: "second", "Augustus", and "moon" or "brilliancy" (=full moon).

This code worked two times is the past 20 years. How it works is that a major earthquake happens somewhere in the world in one year than on the same date, plus or minus one day, the next ("second") year another major earthquake happens on the same date and on a full moon.

Like I just said this code has happen twice in the past 20 years. It happened once in the great Northridge, California earthquake of January 17, 1994. Then on January 16-17, 1995, a year later, in Kobe, Japan another earthquake happen almost to or on the exact date as the first and it was on or near a full moon.

The second time this code has come true was in December 26, 2003 when a major earthquake hit Iran the day after Christmas. Then on December 26, 2004 ("second") another major earthquake hit Asia along with great tidal waves the day after Christmas and that date was a full moon. I actual thought a week before Christmas if we would see another earthquake the day after Christmas in December of 2004.

If this code is correct and the Bible quote and Greek words mean anything then on August 10, 2014, plus or minus three days a major earthquake (and tidal waves?) will hit some where in the world. Another will strike somewhere in the world on August 10, 2013, plus or minus three days, a year earlier.

Song of Solomon 6:10 predicts this second earthquake as happening in the morning, fair moon or full moon, as the sun and as terrible as an army with banners.

"Who is she that looketh forth as the morning, fair as the moon, clear as the sun, and terrible as an army with banners?"
Song of Solomon 6:10 (Old King James Version)

When you look up the word "banners" in the Greek dictionary of the *Strong's Concordance of the Bible* it is near the word for memorial (anniversary). That word means on the anniversary of a past event another events happens on that date connected to when armies come with their flags (=banners) in victory.

Will a major earthquake strike somewhere in the world on August 10, 2013, plus or minus three days, then on August 10, 2014, plus or minus three days another great earthquake strikes somewhere in the world on a full moon ("fair moon")? And that second one is on a Sunday (clear as the sun) and in the morning (=EDT or EST or morning time of the place where the quake hits) on the second anniversary ("banners") of the first one. This is just as Song of Solomon 6:10 and Greek words 4579, 4580,4582, 4572 and Hebrew 226, 234, and 1713 in the *Strong's concordance of the Bible* in the Greek and Hebrew dictionaries predicted. The flag or banners used in these verses and dictionaries can mean a signal or sign of coming danger when armies are approaching. Is that signal of the two armies of the past when Jerusalem was destroyed in July-August of 585 B.C. and 70 A.D.? Will earthquakes, wars, attacks, storms and commotion's such as school shootings or public shootings happen on these dates of July-August in 2013, 2014 and 2018? Are the exact dates from Zechariah 7:3,5 and 8:19 in the fourth and/or fifth month of Av in the Bible's calendar, in which two armies we will see attacked Jerusalem on the same date years apart? The fifth month of Av on the 9th day is when the fast and the two armies attacked Jerusalem. Will on those dates on the 17th of the fourth, or 9th of the fifth, or 19, 21, 26-27, 15 of the seventh month in 2013, 2014 and 2018 we seen again attacks, wars, earthquakes, tidal waves, storms, commotion's and public shootings? Those dates are June 25, July 16-18, 22-24, 2013, August 14-17, 2013, September-October 2013, July 5-7,13-16, 2014, August 2-6, 2014, September-October 2014, July 20-22, 28-31, 2018 and August 19-22, September 19, 21, 26-27 and October of 15 or September-October 2018 or on new moons in those years and months as shown in a latter chapter. The other dates are July 16-17, 2013, 2014, 2018, August 2, 19 and 28-29, 2013, 2014 and 2018 and September 7-8, 19, 26-27, 2013, 2014 and 2018. July 16-17 has several past disasters happen from the sky on those dates. Like TWA flight 800. The comet that hit Jupiter. And JFK, Jr plane crash all happened on those days. August 2, 1990 was the Iraq invasion of Kuwait. August 19 is when Adam was

3

created. And August 28-29 was when satan fell from heaven. And Zechariah 7:1 and 8:19, and Haggai 2:18 tell of the fourth day and 24ᵗʰ day of Chisleu, which is our months of November-December and when Hanukkah is in 518 B.C. and 520 B.C. The *New Living translation* of the Bible tells us that December 7, 518 B.C. was when the fourth day of Chisleu was. That along with Haggai's date when it was written in 520 B.C. equals the Chinese Year of the Snake on December 7, which in 2013 A.D. and is the fourth day from a new moon (December 3). Could December 6-7, 2013 be a time of double trouble and blessings as those books of Haggai and Zechariah predicts? The year 2013 is the Chinese Year of the Snake the same as 520 B.C. See my other book entitled *The Experiment at Philadelphia* for more details of these events. See the book *Armageddon* by Grant Jeffrey for documentation of this fifth month and ninth day when two great armies came and completely destroyed Jerusalem. For the date December 7 see the book *Today's Parallel Bible* with NIV;NASB;KJV;NLT page 2173 and look at the NLT version on that page and notes below.

The "these so many years" of the fifth month and seventh month that Zechariah 7:3,5 predicted the Jewish people fasted and prayed on was from the years 585 B.C. to 515 B.C. In 585 B.C. the Jewish Temple was destroyed on the ninth of Av (fifth month) and was the Chinese Year of the Rat. The polar opposite of the Rat is the Horse that rules 2014 A.D. and 70 A.D. was the Chinese Year of the Horse the same as 2014 A.D. In 515 B.C. the Jewish people had finished rebuilding the Jewish temple and dedicated it. That year is the Chinese Year of the Dog, which 2018 and part of 2019 A.D. is. These same 70 years from 585 B.C. to 515 B.C. are the "many years" predicted of Zechariah 7:3, Daniel and Jeremiah and may also be connected to the same time period to the time of the end as shown in the chapter five.

The moon phases in 518 B.C. when Zechariah chapter 7 was written is very close to the same moon phase as 2013 making the fourth day of the ninth month be December 6-7, 2013 just as I mentioned above. Moon phases are different each year making lunar calendars different each year along with their feasts and fasts days. The moon phase in 515 B.C. is very close to the same moon phase of 2019 when in January 21, 2019 there is a full moon and lunar eclipse. See the book: *Canon of Lunar Eclipses 1500 B.C.-A.D. 3000* by Bao-Lin Liu and Alan D. Fiala. And Zechariah 8:19 predicts the tenth month, which to our calendar is in December-January (=January 21, 2019?), is when something happens.

According to the book *As Above, So below*, by Alan Oken page 157 Emperor Augustus was born September 23, 63 B.C. The year 63 B.C. was the Chinese Year of the Horse the same as 2014 A.D. We get the name August from the name of the Roman Emperor Augustus. We also get the name Sunday from the sun and the full moon from the phase fair moon as Song of Solomon 6:10 predicts. See chapter 7 for names of the days of the week and month's names. On August 10, 2014 is a Sunday, full moon, August and the Chinese Year of the Horse exactly as predicted.

And as Song of Solomon 6:13 predicts the end will come four years (=four returns) after that on August 10 or August 28-29, 2018, or January 21, 2019, which is still the year 2018 to the Chinese calendar?

"Return, return, O Shulamite, return, return, that we may look upon thee. What will ye see in the Shulamite? As it were the company of two armies." Song of Solomon 6:13 (Old King James Version)

The "four returns" of that verse can mean four years added to 2014, which equal 2018 into 2019. The word "return" can mean return to a new year four times or four years later. And the "shulamite" mentioned may be connected to Solomon's name that means "peaceful" and "complete, whole and full under Hebrew words 7999-8004 in the Hebrew Dictionary in the book *Strong's Concordance of the Bible.* The two armies Song of Solomon 6:13 predicts are the two armies that came in July or August in 585- 586 B.C. and 70 A.D. to destroy the Jewish Temple and scatter the Jews. It is called the ninth day of Av, or the month before on the Bible's calendar, and both times those events happened on the same date even though to our calendar it may have been different dates because the Jewish calendar is lunar and ours is solar.

These two earthquakes in August of 2013-2014 might be the only major events of those months of July or August. The wars, terrorist attacks, storms, shootings, volcano eruptions that darkens the skies, famines, pestilence's and other commotion's might come later on as the Bible predicts "by and by" and the beginning of sorrows starts then in 2013-2014. See Luke 21:9 and Matthew 24:8.

CHAPTER TWO

OTHER PREDICTIONS FOR 2013-2014

The flu epidemic of 1918-1919 that killed millions in the Spring of 1918 and peaked in the Fall of 1918 may again happen in those months or December of 2014 into 2015. The years 1918 and 1919 are the Chinese years of the Horse (=2014) and the Year of the Sheep or Goat (=2015). Will we see a new and very deadly form of a flu on those years in which Jesus predicted as a pestilence or epidemic of diseases or flu, which He said would come around when great earthquakes are happening around the world in different (divers) places during a war (=WWI)? See Matthew 24:7:

"For nation shall rise against nation, and kingdom against kingdom, and there shall be famines, and pestilence's, and earthquakes in divers places." Matthew 24:7 (Old King James Version)

The epidemic or pestilence maybe caused by horses, sheep or goats or birds (=Gemini=Horse=2014) and flying

(=Gemini to) things as the Chinese Years of the Horse and Sheep or Goat may predict. Revelation 6:8 predicts a great out break of disease to happen caused by animals. And with the Horse of Chinese astrology being our Gemini sign it could mean birds that the ancient Egyptians believed was connected to the Gemini sign causes this epidemic to start. The world wide epidemic could be for 2018-2019. Read my books of predictions on those years in *Predictions for 2015, 2018 and 2019* coming between now (2011) and December of the year 2012. Will this sicknesses or pestilence's cause sores and fever as Revelation chapter 16 predicts? Or are those predictions of Revelation chapters 6 and 16 that of the "Black death" that hit Europe centuries ago and killed a third of all Europe? Revelation chapters 6 and 16 predicts a quarter of the population killed in which a third is very close to that. Revelation chapter 9 predicts a third of mankind killed by animals carrying disease coming from the bottomless pit where most UFO researchers claim UFOs come from. My book *The antichrist* shows how UFOs are demons coming up out of hell at the center of the earth where there is fire and brimstone. Brimstone can be translated sulfur in which some people claim UFO beings smell like and hell smells like and strange beasts seen on earth smells like (big foot?).

Revelation chapters 6 and 16 predicts people dying with high fever (heat) and black sores on them exactly as Revelation 6 and 16 predicted. It even predicted the disease coming from animal, which the black death was caused by fleas on rats. One cable channel claimed people saw lights in the sky releasing gases into the air and black shadowy figures at the edge of town in the fields (crops-sickle) shortly before the black death appeared. Was the lights UFOs or demons releasing the disease in gas in the sky. The people said shortly after they saw these things people soon began to die. Was the black shadowy figures where we get the term "the grime reaper?" from. And did they cause the black death by UFO beings who we just read are demons from hell at the center of the earth coming up from there (the bottomless pit) just as the book of Revelation predicted. See my book *The experiment at Philadelphia* drawing 6 page 422 for a drawing of the bottomless pit.

Zechariah 9:14 predicts whirlwinds and arrows to hit the south in 2014. In chapter year codes of the Bible Zechariah chapter 9 is our year 2002 A.D. See Chapter 7: The Codes. Add 12 years of the Chinese cycle and it equals 2014 when great whirlwinds (=storms or hurricanes=plural) hit the south in the U.S. The "arrows" predicted in that same verse could mean an terrorist attacks, or bombs, missile or bullets hitting the southern U.S.. Or it could mean a school or public shooting in the south on a Thursday. Our day of Thursday is the blood covenant when Jesus died on the cross on that day as Zechariah 9:11,14 predicts. Are those predictions near or on a new moon (trumpet of verse 14) and when earthquakes and tidal waves, wars, attacks, shootings and storms are about to happen in July-August of 2013-2014 and 2018? The ancient Jewish people sounded a trumpet at the new moon each month and at the time when war was about to happen. The storms or hurricanes and attacks, wars, terrorist attacks and shooting may happen near each other when these earthquake strikes or the other dates given in this book.

Nostradamus in quatrain C6:Q24 predicts a war when Mars (Leo-or Tuesday) and scepter (=Jupiter=Thursday) happens in Cancer. Leo could mean the Leo sign from July 21-23 to August 22-23, plus a cusp of seven to August 28-30. It could also mean a U.S. President born in Leo as President Obama is. The Cancer sign starts on June 21 to July 21-23, 2014 and star time from July 21-23 to August

21-23, 2014, plus the cusp to August 28-30, 2014. In June of 2002 Pakistan and India were on the verge of war in that year, which is the same Chinese Year as 2014. Will we see them again on the verge of war then in 2014 or some other war or attack in July-August of 2013-2014? A strange thing is happening now (July 15, 2011) and that is India has just been attack by someone and they are already threatening to attack Pakistan if they were the attackers. And U.S. President Obama is reporting to make a deal with congress to raise taxes and wants the deal done by August 2, 2011. Add nine, the number of Mars, which we seen in that Nostradamus quatrain, to 2002, the year we seen connected to these ancient prophecies, and it equals 2011 in Leo sign or star time from July 21-September 23+7=30, 2011 or August 2, 19, 28-29, 2011. Is that when this plane crash could happen or the war between India and Pakistan happens? Is this what Daniel 11:19-20 was predicting as a vile man raising taxes and then takes a trip by plane (=eagle) around the world and it crashes into the ocean and his body is never found or hard to find? Both events are in the July-August-September-October time space a few years earlier than 2013-2014. Will they happen now or as Colossians 2:16-17 predicts are a sign of them happening in our future in 2013-2014, 2015, 2016-2018 in those same months, or March-April and in the same ways?

That same plane crash was predicted for President Clinton in April of 1996, but failed to happen. He was from Little Rock, which Obadiah 1-6 predicts a leader from a "small" (=little) and "rock" (=Edom) would fly like an eagle high in the sky (=airplane) and be brought down to the ground. Will this event happen to him sometime in the future or to another U.S. President in the future? Twelve years of Chinese cycles from 1996 equals 2008, plus six years as the polar opposite, equals 2014 when this plane crash with someone famous happens.

The ancient prophecies of that plane crash are predicted in Obadiah 1-6, Psalms chapter 99, Daniel 11:19-25, Zechariah chapter 11, Jeremiah 23:19-20 and 30:23-24 and Amos 2:14. Those predictions are that of an airplane crash with some leader on board and possibly in the ocean and his body never found or hard to find. This airplane crash maybe by accident caused by mechanical failure or by lightning or storm. These ancient prophecies predict an invention failure as Psalms 99:8 predicted for someone who sits between the Cherubs and is leader of a nation spiritually known as Babylon, which could be the U.S., Rome, Italy, Turkey or Iraq. He raises taxes and then takes a trip around the world and his plane goes down in the ocean on the way back. See Daniel 11:19-25. The Cherubs represents the sun that rule the double Pisces zones as the two longitude zones over the eastern U.S. where the White House is and in land. The middle of those zones (=sits between the Cherubs=sun) that go through almost exactly between New York City, Philadelphia and Washington, D.C.

These prophecies could also mean airplanes are again used in terrorists attacks on those cities or Chicago or Los Angeles or the White House. If President Obama is President in 2013 it maybe him at the White House whose attacked. He is born in the Leo sign that is ruled by the sun and Pisces, which rule the cities of Los Angeles, Chicago, Philadelphia, New York City and Washington, D.C. Twelve years added to 9-11-2001 when planes attacked buildings in New York City equals 2013 when they may again strike as Chinese cycles of 12 predicts. Or will this time they attack nuclear power plants or our electricity power source? If a woman is the U.S, President at this time it may be her that these ancient prophecies happen to. There are several prophecies of an end time woman leader of the U.S. See Revelation chapters 17-18; *Unusual prophecies being fulfilled* by Perry Stone page 67;and *The Book Of Angels* by Ruth Thompson, L.A. Williams, and Renae Taylor, pages 116-121. That woman President of the U.S. may come in 2012 or 2016 and be the U.S. President in 2013 and/or 2017 and rule until the end comes.

Chapter Three

The Carving

The ancient Egyptian carving on the ceiling of the temple Hathor in Dendera, Egypt dated 100-300 B.C. or earlier might predict the events in this book. See my book entitled *The Experiment at Philadelphia* page 462 drawing 45 for a look at part of that ancient carving. In it you see a kneeling woman, near three stars, one star, a pig, seven stars, a raft with a goat's head on it and the sun or moon disk between its horns, one star again and a table with four snakes on it. Near that table is a kneeling woman. The woman represents Cancer the woman sign that runs from June 21 to July 21-23 and star time from July 21-23 to August 21-23. Add seven days (=the seven stars) to the August 21-23 and it equals August 28-30.

The pig seen on the carving is the Chinese Year of the Pig which 2007 A.D. is. Add seven years (the seven stars) to the year 2007 and it equals 2014 in June 21 to August 30, which we just seen the kneeling woman meant. Add the four snakes seen on the carving near the pig to 2014 and it equals 2018. The snakes can also mean the Chinese Year of the Snake, which is 2013, plus one star (one year) added to that, and four years more as the four snakes, and it equals 2013+1=2014+4=2018. The polar opposite of Snake in Chinese astrology is the Pig. And the kneeling woman in Chinese astrology equals our Cancer sign and July and is ruled by the Chinese Sheep or Goat, which head (goat's head on a raft=waters=Cancer sign) is seen next to the kneeling woman on that carving. From these calculations we can conclude that on June 21-August 30, 2013, 2014, 2015, 2016 and 2018 certain events may happen then as documented in this book.

Chapter Four

The Trumpets and Sun

The word "trumpet" or "trumpets" are predicted six times in the book of Revelation. Could this have been a prediction of some event or events happening on a new moon in which we seen the ancient Jewish people would sound a trumpet at the sight of a new moon or right after it? The new moons in June 21-August 30, 2013, 2014 and 2018 are July 8, 2013 and August 6, 2013 and June 27, 2014, July 26, 2014, August 25, 2014, July 12-13, 2018 and August 11, 2018. May 28, 2014 is also a new moon as well as November 22, 2014. Are these dates when a great earthquake strikes San Francisco and/or Seattle with possible tidal waves or a great earthquake and tidal waves strike somewhere in the world?

Revelation chapter 5 predicts a small book with seven seals (=seven chapters) to be open by the "Lamb" from the tribe of Juda and root of David. The "Lamb" is a sheep or goat in which we seen Chinese astrology rules our Cancer sign and month of July. It also is the star time of Cancer when certain events may happen in from July 21-23 to

August 21-23. The tribe of Juda the lion equals Leo the lion sign that runs from July 21- 23 to August 22-23, plus seven day cusp to August 28-30. Leo the lion is ruled by our sun, which rules the eastern U.S. and possibly the Sun tabloid and National Enquirer. The "root of David" is David's father Jesse who was born in the Cancer sign. Were these ancient prophecies predicting a seven chapter book to be open by David (Perel?) or Jesse, John or Ed in the Sun and/or National Enquirer tabloids on the dates mentioned in 2013, 2014 or 2018? Is the "lamb" that opens the seven chapter book might be born on April 6 or 9, the dates of Jesus's death and resurrection (the slain lamb in Revelation chapter 5)? Or is he born on June 24-25 (Jesus's birthday), or on June 27, which is Jesse's birthday the father or root of David? Or is it June 20 the birthday of John the Disciple of Jesus who wrote down the Bible's book of Revelation in heaven on June 12, 96 A.D., which was a Sunday the same as August 10, 2014. And David's birthday the father of Solomon was September 7-8, 19 or 26-27 and Solomon's birthday was October 15. July 19 is the ancient Egyptian New Year, which could be the birthday of this editor. The lion (Leo) from the tribe of Juda that Revelation 5:5 predicts could be the editor or leader of the Sun and/or National Enquirer birth sign or star sign of July 21-September 23, plus or minus the cusp of seven days to September 30 or July 14. Are any of these names and birthdays connected to the Sun or National Enquirer? Will one of them named above or born on the above dates help open or publish an excerpt of this seven chapter book (seven seals) in the seventh month (September-October) of 2013?

You may ask what in the world does a seven sealed book opened in heaven have to do with a seven chapter book opened on earth? Psalms 84:11 states God in heaven is a sun and the Sun tabloid on earth is not only in the sunshine state of Florida, but in the Pisces zone that rules the sun and the tabloid is called the Sun. And if they decide to publish an excerpt from this book of seven chapters (=seven seals) they would open (publish or go public) one or more seals from this book when no one else would just as Revelation chapter 5 predicts they would. Revelation 1-5 states that God and the lamb in heaven shine as the strength of the sun (=Sun tabloid). And Revelation chapter 5 predicts two sevens, which could mean twice is this book excerpt published in July-August or later in 2013 and in July-August or later in 2014. The seven churches that the book of Revelation was sent to long ago were in western Turkey which was the end of the Virgo zone and near the beginning of the Libra zone. The great pyramids below them are exactly on the Virgo-Libra zones. Is that when Revelation's small book is opened (published) in the Sun or National Enquirer? The end of Virgo and beginning of the Libra sign is from September 14-23, plus the cusp of seven days to September 30, or into Libra, which runs from September 23-October 22. The ancient Egyptian New Year where the great pyramids were built as a starting point began on July 19, which is when some of these events in this book may happen on.

The "little book" that Revelation chapters 4-5-10 predict could mean a small 5x8 paperback written on the front and back of each page with seven chapters as those prophecies predict for this book. In ancient times books were large and only written on one side and so these prophecies were predicting a modern day book.

CHAPTER FIVE

THE END

The count down to the end was predicted by Hal Lindsey as a starting point when Israel (fig tree) became a nation again on May 14-15, 1948. See his book *The Late Great Planet Earth*. He claims the "fig tree" represents Israel and is the sign for the count down of the last generation. Matthew 24:32-34 predicts this:

"Now learn a parable of the fig tree; When his branch is yet tender, and putteth forth leaves, ye know that the summer is nigh.

So likewise ye, when ye see all these things, know that it is near, even at the doors.

Verily I say unto you. This generation shall not pass, till all these things be fulfilled." Matthew 24:32-34 (Old King James Version).

The summer being "nigh" may predict the end in summer time as the months of July-August are. And the "generation" might be 70 years as Psalms 90:10 predicts for a life time that David the king of Israel (fig tree) is strongly connected to. Add 70 years to May 14-15, 1948 and come to May 14-15, 2018 when the signs come for the end sometime in summer.

The fig tree puts forth leaves and fruits in the spring and summer. *The Smith's Bible dictionary* on pages 192-193 states that the fruit always comes before the leaves and the figs harvest is in May-June the same month Israel became a nation.

The "sorrows" that Matthew 24:8 predicts as signs of the count down to the end Hal Lindsey claims that word can be translated "birth pangs." Virgo the Virgin in astrology and numerology is a woman and is given the number five. If the commotion's happened in 2013-2014 and you add five years to those years it equals 2018-2019. Matthew 24:7 predicts those commotion's as wars, pestilence's and famines in verse seven then the very next verse eight it predicts that they would be signs of the sorrows to come as birth pangs of a woman giving birth. Does those ancient prophecies mean the commotion's or attacks on 9-11-2001? And then two years (by and by=Luke 21:9) later the great second Iraq war happened. That war involved nation against nation, and kingdom against kingdom in a great war with great signs and fearful sights from heaven (=shock and awe). The shock and awe are the fearful and great signs from heaven that happened then causing earthquakes, famines and pestilence's in 2003, but it is not the end or the end is not in September 26-27, 2003 as Luke 21:9-11 predicted. Twelve years added to that date is September 26-27, 2015 when certain events may happen on.

Does the four returns of Song of Solomon 6:13 predict four years from when the earthquake happens on August 10, 2014 till the end in August 28-29, 2018? In my other books I show how in 26 A.D. was when John the Baptist and Jesus came proclaiming the kingdom of God is at hand. The Chinese Year of 26 A.D. is the Year of the Dog the same as 2018 and part of 2019 A.D. are. And Daniel 12:11-12 prediction of 1290 days and 1335 days added together equals 2625 days. Change each day to years as Ezekiel 4:6 tells us to do and you have 2625 years. Daniel 12:11-13 tells us to start the count down from when the king of Babylon came and stopped the daily sacrifice and did the abomination by standing in or putting a pagan statue in the Holy of Holies in the Jewish Temple at Jerusalem. The Book of Daniel starts at this time in Chapter one of that book in the third year of Jehoiakim, which was 606-607 B.C. Subtract 2625 days from then and it equals 2019-2020. Counting each year it equals 2018-2019 A.D. as the time of the end. Here's what the book of Daniel 12:11-12 prediction states:

"And from thew time that the daily sacrifice shall be taken away, and the abomination that maketh desolate set up, there shall be a thousand two hundred and ninety days.

Blessed is he that waiteth, and cometh to the thousand three hundred and five and thirty days." Daniel 12:11-12.

The vision that I had on August 29, 1982 at 1:18 am to 7:18 am-a Sunday, of God as a Cherub for almost exactly six hours might give the year and date of the end. Six (hours) times six equals 36 hours or years. Add 36 years to 1982 and it equals 2018 at 1:18 a.m. on August 29 as the end of days that Daniel predicted the end would come when many travel to and fro for their summer vacations, which happens mostly in July-August according to *The Travel Channel*.

In the book of Revelation and other parts of the Bible there is often mentioned the wrath of God happening in the end as wine or the vine harvest, winepress or grapes and vineyards. The grapes used for making wine come from a vine and are their harvest is from August-September and some have even claimed is from June to September as the harvest for grapes. See *Holman Bible Dictionary* page 610. Was this a clue for the end in July-August of 2018? Or is the half hour (=half a year=six months) from then till the months of January-February of 2019 is when the end comes? See Revelation 8:1 for the half an hour prediction. Is the half hour of Revelation 8:1 a prediction of 30 minutes, dropping the zero, equals three minutes or three years as the same three angels of Revelation chapter 14 come at the end when the wrath of the wine press of God happens? Are those three years July-August of 2013, 2014 and 2015 or 2018?

CHAPTER SIX

COME TO CHRIST

Forget about what the antichrist and false prophet say and write, which I showed in the first 14 chapters of my book *The Experiment in Philadelphia*, if they come. What they say will poison the mind. But fear God and keep His commandments just as Solomon wrote in Ecclesiastics 12:13-14. Jesus said if you love Him you will keep His commandments. See John 14:15. He also said He is the truth and the life and the only way to the Father and heaven. He is purely the Son of God and perfect in every way and righteous. All of us have failed in our life, some many times, and in many ways. Maintaining a balance of the two, as the antichrist may teach, is also wrong as Jesus taught in Revelation 3:16. He said, regarding those who are lukewarm (balance), that Jesus will vomit out of his mouth anyone and any church that is that way. Yet Jesus gives us a second chance at life. What a great and beautiful thing that is!

The second chance comes when you are ready to repent of your sins, ask Jesus into your heart and life and live His ways for the rest of your life. Say this simple prayer and mean it with all your heart:

> Dear Jesus: I repent of all my sins. Please forgive me for all the sins I have committed in my life. Come into my life and heart and be my Savior and Lord and I will live for you forever. Amen.

Imagine this: after you said that prayer all the mistakes you ever made in life are forgiven completely. There will be no more fear, shame or guilt or remembrance of them ever again. This is because the blood of Jesus dying on the cross has saved you and given you that new freedom from those things bothering you ever again. You have a new life in Jesus and can live and die knowing that and have no fear of past sins or death and hell. You are born again!

Change your lifestyle after you said that prayer and live for Jesus. Go to a Bible-based church every Sunday. Pray every day. Read the Bible everyday. Do not sin and keep all the laws of the land. When you get this second chance do not waste it or throw it away because it is precious. Love Jesus and worship Him every day and live for Him. Most of all, keep the two greatest commandments, which is to love God with all your mind, soul and heart and most of all love your neighbor as yourself. You will find a loving good friend in Jesus when these things are done. Pray for the baptism in the Holy Ghost and tell others of Jesus. Give copies of this book and my other books to others as witnessing tools. See the web site: WWW.Authorhouse.COM for all my books and future ones to come and it will tell you how to order them. Separate yourself from the world for the world is not friendly with the ways of God. And remember, no one or things can take your salvation away. God bless all of you now and forever. Amen.

A few things should be stated about Christianity today. Do not point the finger at other people's sins, point the finger at you. Judge yourselves and not others or people even those in authority. Judge not lest ye be judged. Examine yourselves and not others. See Luke 6:37, Jude 8-11 and Matthew 7:1-5. Sinners will see the positive light in you and follow Jesus. I know the Bible says to tell people of their sins, but it also says these things just mentioned. When Jesus was here He never judged the sinners, but judged very hard the religious leaders for their judgement of others over every little thing. The Holy Bible says not to bring up other people's sins. Jude says that even the archangel Michael didn't accused the Devil of anything when over a dispute over the body of Moses. If he doesn't judge the Devil himself how much more should we not judge people.

Do not give to get. That is the wrong way to teach people to give. I know the Bible verses that teach those things, but I also know the Bible says to give and not to expect back. See Luke 6:29-30 and Matthew 10:5-42. Freely you were given your gifts and freely you should give them to others not for money. See Matthew 10:5-42.

Do not come to Christ for prosperity, success, fame and power as many teach today. Come to Christ humbly and without these motivations or expectations. Christianity can be very difficult if followed correctly. See Matthew 10:5-42. Family and friends can turn against you. Living without the world as your god and all the sins it brings can be extremely difficult to give up. This is why James said be not friendly with the world because it is at enmity with God. See James 4:4.

Beware of Eastern religions and all other religions and spirituality movements no matter how good they sound for they are not from God, but are ancient Gentile gods who are devils as explained in my book *The Antichrist* as MYSTERY

BABYLON. There were only Ten Commandments in the Bible and you know what the first one is? It's not do not murder, or do not steal, or do not commit adultery, as important as those commandments are and are of the ten. The first commandment was "to have no other gods before me (The Jewish God the one and only true God). God wouldn't of said that if there weren't other gods and wouldn't of put it at the beginning of the Ten Commandments if it were not very important. Look at all the trouble today in the world. The trouble is not true Christianity! Its other gods and other religions, which God explained in the Bible as devils (=gods). See my book *The Antichrist* for more details of those other gods.

People in this generation don't want to hear "the devil made me do it" or "the devil told me to do it" as it is so far and hard to believe these horrible killers telling us that is what really happened. Yet this generation loves to blame God for everything. The BTK serial killer claimed demons drove him to do it. And everyone mocked that answer. Another family member found several of his victims and he said when he found them brutally murdered he right then and there "lost his religion." Like God did it instead of demons. One famous hit song in the past was called "losing my religion." One person once said when trouble occurs it either drives people away from God or nearer to Him. And believing is everything. It's the mighty power in good and it is the mighty power in evil, just believing. Believing can change your life and keep you out of hell or it can bring you down to hell forever. That's why Jesus taught so much about faith and believing in the Bible. It is also why the Bible calls Christians believers and non Christians unbelievers.

In the past four decades we seen God, prayer, the Bible, Nativity scenes and Ten Commandments removed from our schools, public buildings and court houses. What have we seen ever since? A great murderous killings in schools, public buildings and courthouses. God is not mocked. He is not just sitting back while you take Him out of everything. If you don't want God in these places and things He will let the Devil and great lawlessness come in and that is exactly what happened. You got your wish of not having God in these places and now you have the Devil. But you say don't blame the Devil for those great murders, but you blame God. But you don't believe in God? What is your excuse then? This generation is like Romans 1:22 claims as "professing to be wise became fools."

Questions have raised as to whether the U.S. is a Christian nation and if Christianity should be allowed in any part of it especially public and federal buildings. The lawyers have gotten so many confused about this. A little girl was thrown out of school for saying grace. When Bibles or Jesus are not allowed to be read or spoken of to anyone or by anyone in public and federal places, is that freedom? That's a simple question. Is that freedom? Is it? NO!!! And we all will agree this nation was founded on just that--freedom. When you offend atheists by Nativity scenes, Bibles and Christianity and take them away what about the Christian's rights who you then offend?

Just Look at whom you elected President of the U.S.? You elected President Obama, who he and his wife are ashamed of the U.S. He goes over to Europe and makes friends with all of our enemies and blasts the U.S. for being proud. He, or one of his spokesmen, said the U.S. is not a Christian nation or founded on Christianity. Even a democratic news anchorperson said what would our enemies think of us with him saying such things? The latest poll in Israel says only eight percent of Israelis like President Obama. That makes 92 percent of Israelis who dislike him. He promise to be good friend with Israel before he was elected and the first day in office he gave an interview to an Arab TV network that shows captured Americans being beheaded by terrorist. President Obama refused nation prayer day to have any Christian preacher come into the White House to pray on a certain day which many U.S. Presidents have done on that day for decades. He never invited Billy Graham to the White House who's been in the audience of every U.S. President since the 1950's or 1960's. Yet on the Muslin Holy Day President Obama had a big party and celebration at the White House.

One neighbor I witness to about Jesus Christ said that if Jesus were born today He would be a bastard. I tried to tell them He was virgin born, but they mocked that. Such blasphemy! After I got done witnessing to them I said even if I am wrong do you want to take a chance on going to hell? Before I even finished the sentence he answered in a quick strong angry voice, Yes! Yes he will take the chance.

One man I was talking to about being born again said he liked a bumper sticker he saw that said: "I was born right the first time." I immediately thought of Paul's writing in the Bible that the preaching of the cross and salvation is utter foolishness to the unbeliever. You just can't understand why the whole world is foolish in Christianity and you are right can you?

One man I met once said he couldn't believe in a God that let his wife slip in and out of consciousness during Child labor. The man said that it is right there in the Bible that God would make women suffer during childbirth. And it is, but is that any reason to hate your creator or not to believe in Him?

Another man I met I said to him "have a Merry Christmas." Before I could even get the finished sentence out of my mouth he said back: "I'll have a merry Santa Claus Christmas!" He didn't even want the mention of Christmas just like many don't want Nativity scenes at Christmas time. What in God's name is the world coming to? These things are such hatred of God from this perverse and twisted generation. People quote Lennon the evil Russian leader, or Karl Marx, the founder of atheistic communism, long ago over his saying of how sickening religion is. And people today love *The Da Vinci Code* book that mocks and blasphemies God.

People who say the Bible is contradicting, vague and has inconsistencies are just ignorant. If they had any knowledge of it they wouldn't say those things. In one of my books remember me saying that I wondered at people who say things about the Bible and wonder how much research and study they did on it. The answers are always none. They say these things simply because they feel that way, not because of study and research. Let's throw our feelings out the window and look for solid truth to these things. Let's not base important things and decisions on feelings.

It is easy to knock something, but hard to prove it. I am sick of seeing Skeptic Magazine editor or owner on TV knocking prophecy. Anyone can do that. That is very easy. Why don't you try to prove it instead of saying it is vague and self- fulfilling prophecies when prophecy does come true? They all say the Bible is so vague or could be made to say anything and they put no stock into prophecy. Then when a detail prophecy comes true they say a coincidence or self fulfilling, meaning if you say you will get the flu on February 18 you will get the flu on that date because it's self fulfilling. Give me a break! You have no knowledge of prophecy so don't speak cause you ignorance shows. If you say enough times an earthquake is about to happen is that self-fulfilling? Then they say quickly "well there always been earthquakes." If a storm is prophesied and it happens is it a wild coincidence or self fulfilling because there always been storms? This type of thinking is not wise, but stupid. The study of Bible prophecy for the first Coming of Christ alone is amazing. All those details can't be vague or coincidence or self-fulfilling. See study Bibles in the rear for a list of those prophecies and Hal Lindsey's book The Late Great Planet Earth. Judas could of betrayed Jesus for any number of pieces of silver, but it was predicted 30. Jesus could have been born any other place, but Bethlehem, but was as predicted. His parents didn't even live in Bethlehem. You can go on and on about the many predicted events of Christ's first Coming. Read the list of them and their fulfillment's in those sources I just gave. You will be just amazed. See the Ryrie Study Bible pages 1879-1882.

Let me say something about TV preachers and your local preachers. And that is a few may be phonies and many may have sin in their life like we all do, but they are the only ones preaching Jesus Christ. They lead people to repent of their sins and accept Jesus Christ as Lord and Savior and to read the Bible, pray and go to Church. Do you do that? Does your family or friends do that? Do the people you watch or listen to on TV or radio or CD, movies, books or whatever do that? NO!!! If you took a survey of the people in all churches I think you will find a great many are there in church directly or indirectly by the TV preachers teaching them so. Jesus' Disciples came to Him one time and said they caught someone doing something in Jesus name and they forbid him not to do that. Jesus told them forbid them not for those who are with me are not against me.

Another note: The mystery Babylon as described in my other books as the birth of the Gentiles from women devils mating with Jewish men was true and not the antichrist writing. It is now made known as Romans 16:25-27 and Malachi 4:6 claimed for the obedience of faith for all. It was made known so the fathers (Jewish) love their sons

(Gentiles) and the sons (Gentiles) love their fathers (Jewish) just as Malachi 4:6 predicted. So go in faith, obedience and love among all races both now and forever. See my other book *The Antichrist*.

A final note: At the end of this world and when the Second Coming of Christ happens there could be great storms, wars, volcanoes, earthquakes and other troubles happening in the world, but then it may not be. That year or two or three years before or a month or two before may see peace treaties, not many storms or earthquakes, a SDI system deployed, prosperity and many saying Peace, Peace and Peace and safety. Then one day many will be looking up to see a strange light by the Sun and soon after our Sun novas and the end. See Jeremiah chapter 6; I Thessalonians 5:3; Luke 21:25-36; Matthew 24:37-42. Is the saying of "Peace, Peace or Peace and safety" a prediction of two years of peace from 2012 or 2016, then a very great and sudden destruction? If President Obama reaches a Peace Treaty with Israel and the Palestinians between now and 2012-2013 or 2014-2016 then watch out for sudden destruction. The great antichrist was predicted to come and make peace then he starts an awful war. Was that prediction that of a Peace Treaty with the state of Israel and the Palestinians then war or sudden destruction? Or does it mean now with President Obama winning the Nobel Peace prize and then in 2010 attacks or helps Israel attack Iran then a tremendous war breaks out? That's exactly what the Bible predicted the antichrist to do all along. I don't think it is wrong for President Obama to help Israel to attack Iran, I think it is right. But what will happen after that attack is the big question. In these end times reverse is true of some things. You can do right and still be wrong and you can do wrong and be right. But as I said earlier the end time antichrist doesn't have to come cause all was fulfilled in WWII in Hitler.

Today many lay and wait for some TV preacher or local preacher or some Christian to fall to some sin and they then accuse them as being hypocrites and why they don't follow Christ and Christianity. That's just the point! Follow Christ and not Christians, men, women and children. If you put your trust in them they are sure to fall. But if you put your trust in Christ He will never fall. Read the four gospels of the New Testament and see for yourself how perfect Christ was His whole life. People will always let you down, but Christ will never let you down. Put your trust in His righteousness and not in peoples' righteousness.

But remember Jesus Christ is the true meaning of life and not vanity or emptiness. He loves you deeply and wants you to accept Him as Lord and savior. Come to Christ…

Amen!

Chapter Seven

The Codes

The following astrology, numerology, Chinese astrology and other information applies to the codes used in this book to predict the dates, places, times, names and etc:

Aries: head, March 21-April 20.
Taurus: neck, April 20-May 20.
Gemini: arms, May 21-June 20.
Cancer: breasts, June 21-July 22.
Leo: heart, July 23-August 22.
Virgo: belly, August 23-September 22.
Libra: reins (kidneys), September 23-October 22.
Scorpio: secret parts (sex), October 23-November 21.
Sagittarius: thighs, November 22-December 21.
Capricorn: knees, December 22-January 19.
Aquarius: legs, January 20-February 19.
Pisces: feet, February 20-March 20.

Note: The cusp of each sign above is a seven day period

added or subtracted to the end or beginning of each sign in which that sign also rules in.

Star time of the 12 signs:

Aries: April 20-May 20
Taurus: May 21-June 20
Gemini: June 21-July 22
Cancer: July 23-August 22
Leo: August 23-September 22
Virgo: September 23-October 22
Libra: October 23-November 21
Scorpio: November 22-December 21
Sagittarius: December 22-January 19
Capricorn: January 20-February 19
Aquarius: February 20-March 20
Pisces: March 21-April 19

Note: Due to the movement of the equinoxes the original 12 signs has moved in relationship to the Sun from when they were first set about 2000 years ago. I call this star time meaning when the Sun (star) is in that sign. The list above this one shows the times when the Sun was in those 12 signs about 2000 years ago. Now they are about 30 degrees difference to when the Sun is in each sign. About 2160 years from now they will be 30 degrees more difference then now. This is why I say the sphinx is the symbol of 0 degrees Virgo 30 degrees Leo at the summer solstice because it was a symbol of or built when the Sun on June 21 (summer solstice) was at about 0 degrees Virgo 30 degrees Leo. Today, of course, the Sun is at another position. It is also why October 31 nowadays can mean August 29 long ago with the Sun's movement through the signs. Time changes can also be due to the change in calendars as we will see, making September 11 be also August 29 by the old style calendar.

Aries: is ruled by Mars and is given the number 9.
Taurus: is ruled by Venus and is given the number 6.
Gemini: is ruled by Mercury and is given the number 5.
Cancer: is ruled by the Moon and is given the numbers 2-7.
Leo: is ruled by the Sun and is given the numbers 1-4.
Virgo: is ruled by Mercury and is given the number 5.
Libra: is ruled by Venus and is given the number 6.
Scorpio: is ruled by Mars and is given the number 9.
Sagittarius: is ruled by Jupiter and is given the number 3.
Capricorn: is ruled by Saturn and is given the number 8.
Aquarius: is ruled by Saturn and is given the number 8.
Pisces: is ruled by Jupiter and is given the number 3.

Note: Some astrology books lists these signs and planets in slightly different ways in times and ruler-ships. You may want to learn those ways as well. See other astrology books for more information.

Sun: 1-4
Moon: 2-7
Mercury: 5
Venus: 6
Earth:
Mars: 9
Wormwood: 5
Jupiter: 3
Saturn: 8
Uranus: 4
Neptune: 7
Pluto:

1. Aries (ram)
2. Taurus (bull)
3. Gemini (twins)
4. Cancer (crab)
5. Leo (lion)
6. Virgo (Virgin)
7. Libra (scales)
8. Scorpio (scorpion)
9. Sagittarius (archer)
10. Capricorn (sea goat)
11. Aquarius (water bearer)
12. Pisces (fishes)

1. Pisces=Sun
2. Aries=Mercury
3. Taurus=Venus
4. Gemini=Earth
5. Cancer=Moon
6. Leo=Mars
7. Virgo=Wormwood (Satan was literally this star's core).
8. Libra=Jupiter
9. Scorpio=Saturn
10. Sagittarius=Uranus
11. Capricorn=Neptune
12. Aquarius=Pluto

Note: The list above is the other numbers of the 12 signs when starting from the first sign of Pisces instead of Aries. The Pisces sign is the Sun and the number 1 or first sign. This lines up with the 10 planets our Moon and the Sun to the 12 signs.

Polar opposites:
Aries=Libra
Taurus=Scorpio
Gemini=Sagittarius
Cancer=Capricorn
Leo=Aquarius
Virgo=Pisces

Male: Female:
Aries Taurus
Gemini Cancer
Leo Virgo
Libra Scorpio
Sagittarius Capricorn
Aquarius Pisces

Air: Water: Fire: Earth:
Libra Scorpio Aries Taurus
Aquarius Cancer Leo Capricorn
Gemini Pisces Sagittarius Virgo

The ages of humans that the planets rule:

Moon=birth to 4 years old
Mercury=5-14 years old
Venus=14-21 years old
Sun=23-41 years old
Mars=42-56 years old
Jupiter=57-68 years old
Saturn=68 to physical death
Uranus=none
Neptune=none
Pluto=death to birth

Aries: ruled by Mars in a positive aspect.
Taurus: ruled by Venus in a positive aspect.
Gemini: ruled by Mercury in a positive aspect.
Cancer: ruled by the Moon.
Leo: ruled by the Sun.
Virgo: ruled by Mercury in a negative aspect.
Libra: ruled by Venus in a negative aspect.
Scorpio: ruled by Mars in a negative aspect.
Sagittarius: ruled by Jupiter in a positive aspect.
Capricorn: ruled by Saturn in a positive aspect.
Aquarius: ruled by Saturn in a negative aspect.
Pisces: ruled by Jupiter in a negative aspect.

Planets, Sun and Moon as male or female:

Male: Female:
Sun Moon
Mercury Venus
Earth Saturn
Mars Neptune
Jupiter Uranus
Pluto Wormwood

Note: The planet wormwood was a planet between Mars and Jupiter that Satan was before he fell. When he fell he blew up that planet and the asteroid belt is now the remains of it. Comets could also be the remains of it as well. It is interesting to note that when Wormwood blew up around the conception or birth of the antichrist long ago it would take about seven years to reach the earth. That is when the first destruction of the earth after the first week when the first antichrist was a young child (see Isaiah 14) as described in an earlier chapter.

Virgo: Rules reptiles/dinosaurs created by Satan who was Wormwood, which is Virgo.

12 Disciples:

1.Peter=Aries
2.James=Taurus
3.John=Gemini
4.Andrew=Cancer
5.Philip=Leo
6.Bartholomew=Virgo
7.Matthew=Libra
8.Thomas=Scorpio
9.James=Sagittarius
10.Thaddaeus=Capricorn
11.Simon=Aquarius
12.Judas=Pisces=Virgo=Wormwood the planet of Satan who betrayed God originally.

Cities, areas and nations ruled by:

Aries: Texas, Mid-West U.S.
Taurus: Los Angeles, Los Vegas.
Gemini: San Francisco, Seattle, part of England.
Cancer: New York City, part of London and England.
Leo: Jerusalem, Rome, Damascus, Philadelphia, Chicago, L.A.
Virgo: Jerusalem, Baghdad, Iraq, Boston, Kuwait, Greece, Egypt.
Libra: Japan, part of Iraq, Israel, part of Egypt.
Scorpio: Washington, D.C., Iran, part of Iraq.
Sagittarius: Japan, Afghanistan, Pakistan, India.
Capricorn: Korea.

Aquarius: China
Pisces: Eastern U.S.

Note: See the world map in an atlas or book that has the 15 degree longitude for the 24 time zones for each of the 12 signs that rules those areas repeated twice. Start at 75 degrees longitude over or near New York City or Philadelphia as the two back to back Pisces' zones. Then go out in opposite directions counting each 15 degrees as one sign starting with Aries-Aries then Taurus-Taurus and so on till you reach the double Aquarius zones back to back over China. Some cities, areas and nations are ruled by other signs as well. They don't always have to be in those longitude zones to be ruled by a certain sign. For example, New York City is in the middle of the two Pisces zones on a map of longitude, but above is listed to be ruled by Cancer as well. The cusp and star time can change these 24 zones and the signs they rule. Korea, for example, could be in the Sagittarius zone star time instead of Capricorn sign.

Stones:

Beryl=Venus and Gemini
Jasper=Scorpio and Mars
Brass=Venus
Pearls=Moon
Gold=Leo-Sun

Plants:

Frankincense and Myrrh=Sun and Aquarius
Lily=Moon
Pumkins=Moon

<u>Trees</u>:

Palm=Sun
Olive=Moon
Fig=Venus-Libra=the tree of knowledge of good and evil

<u>The four seasons</u>:

<u>Spring</u>: Vernal Equinox (=equal days and nights; the nights are as about long as the day; about 12 hours of light and 12 hours of dark)

<u>Summer</u>: summer solstice (solstice means the sun has stood still; possibly after the first time the earth stopped rotating when the first beast or antichrist was born on June 20-21-22 long ago). The summer solstice is the longest day of the year. From that day the days become shorter till the winter solstice, the shortest day. From the winter solstice the days then become longer till the summer solstice and repeat the cycle.

<u>Fall</u>: Autumn equinox (equals days and nights)

<u>Winter</u>: Winter solstice (shortest day of the year)

<u>The four Cherubim</u>:

1. Lion=Leo=Autumn Equinox

2. Calf=Taurus=Summer Solstice

3. Face of a man=Aquarius=Vernal Equinox

4. Eagle=Aquila=Winter Solstice

Jesus Christ the Son=the planet Venus the bright and morning star and is the air or wind sign. See Revelation 22:16.

Son of man=earth and waters.

Father or Holy Ghost=Mars=god of war and fire.

All other planets and moons and the Sun are governed by Cherubs and angels. See Psalms 104:4-5; Revelation 12.

Sun spots activity maximum:

About every 11 years Sun spots have their greatest activity, but as short as 7 years or as long as 17 years is possible. A peak activity was recorded in 1991-1992. But other years are possible and we seen great activity in sunspots in the fall of 2003. It disturbed satellites, TV, radio and phone receptions.

Sun rotation:

Every 26-28 days near equator different in other latitudes: 27 days is possible, which we seen is a date in prophccy.

Moon's month sidereal, synodic and Moon phases:

Synodic month: 29 1/2 days: from new moon to new Moon.

Sidereal month: 27 1/3=360 degrees, but needs two more days to get to the same phase.

New Moon: Moon completely dark.

Crescent Moon: waxing is two days after a new Moon in western twilight. Waxing means to grow larger or more of the Moon is lighted.

First quarter: about 7-8 days after a new Moon.

Full Moon: about 15 days after a new Moon.

Fourth quarter: about 7-8 days after a full Moon.

Crescent Moon: waning is two days before a new Moon. Waning means become smaller as the lighted part of the Moon is seen.

Note: The Jewish people start their new Moon about a day or two after we in the U.S. starts ours.

Venus' day: 243 days reversed: rotates opposite then our earth. It rotates clockwise and morning is evening and evening is morning.

Venus' year: 225 days

Mars' day: 24 hours 37 minutes

Mars' year 687 days

Jupiter's day: 9 hours 50 minutes

Jupiter's year: 11.9 years

Saturn's day: 10 hours 40 minutes

Saturn's year: 29 1/2 years

Uranus' day: 17 hours 14 minutes

Uranus' year: 84 years

Neptune's day: 16 hours 6 minutes

Neptune's year: 164 years

Pluto's day: 6 days 9 hours?

Pluto's year: 248 years

The new planet or comet or asteroid discovered in 2003 or 2004?

The ages:

Small age: 2,160 years solstices and equinoxes move through one sign. (=72 years x30 degrees=2,160; this works out to 72 years a degree).

One age: 6,480 years solstices and equinoxes move through three signs (=2,160 years times three signs=6,480 years).

Great age: 25,920 years solstices and equinoxes move through the 12 signs (=6,480 years times four ages=25,920 years).

Note: These ages is what is known as the precession of the equinoxes. Why this is, is because the earth not only rotates and goes around the Sun it also spins like a top. When it does this over many years it causes the Sun to move slowly through the 12 signs and makes different North stars. Today our North Star is Polaris. At the time of the pyramids the North Star was Thuban in Draco. In our future the North Pole will be pointing near the feet of Cepheus the king on the throne. Is that the time of the great white throne judgement as Revelation predicted? This is also why we have star time. When the 12 Zodiac signs were set back about 2000 years ago the Sun entered Libra about September 23. Today it enters Libra about October 22, a full 30 days later. Plus or minus 2160 years from now, or before 159 B.C., and you would have still different times when the Sun enters each sign. These things explains why the Sphinx and pyramids can mean Leo-Virgo on the summer solstice as the birth of the antichrist and another as Kephren born in May long ago, about 30 days difference. Today the summer solstice is in Taurus-Gemini. The ancient Egyptians knew of these changes and even predicted things with our North star Polaris (symbol of the Dog or Jackal to the Egyptians) even though in their time the North star may have been Thuban. The sphinx is also possibly the conception date of Kephren on August 19-23-29 long ago making his birthday on May 29. The ancients originally believed that your astrology sign should be at the time of conception. But they knowing that date would be hard to find put the signs at the time of birth. Both births and conceptions times and dates and places are important to your horoscope. To find your conception day or near it count backwards by about 280 days. If you were over due and premature those dates will be different. Plus you may never know the exact date of conception, especially the hour. But they are important. The place you were born is also your sign along with the day of week and polar opposites of your birth and conception dates. Remember the place of birth and place and time of conception can be the 24-hour time zones or the longitude zones with the 12 signs in them.

Meanings of the days of the week:

Sunday=Sun=1-4
Monday=Moon=2-7
Tuesday=Mars=9
Wednesday=Mercury=5
Thursday=Jupiter=3
Friday=Venus=6
Saturday=Saturn=8

The Jewish week: The Christian week:

1. Sunday 1. Monday
2. Monday 2. Tuesday
3. Tuesday 3. Wednesday
4. Wednesday 4. Thursday
5. Thursday 5. Friday
6. Friday 6. Saturday
7. Saturday 7. Sunday

The Jewish Sabbath:

Sunset Friday to Sunset Saturday

The Christian Sabbath:

Midnight Sunday morning to Midnight Monday morning.

The days of the weeks to our 12 signs:

Sunday=Pisces, 1-4.
Monday=Cancer, 2-7.
Tuesday=Aries, 9.
Wednesday=Virgo, 5.
Thursday=Jupiter, 3.
Friday=Taurus, 6.
Saturday=Scorpio, 8.

Meanings of the months names:

January=Roman god Janus, protector of the gates.
February=Latin "to cleanse".
March=Roman god of war, Mars.
April=Latin "to open (bud)".
May=Roman goddes Maia.
June=Roman goddess Juno or youth.
July=Julius Ceasar.
August=Augustus Ceasar.
September=Latin seven.
October=Latin eight.
November=Latin nine.
December=Latin ten.

Full Moon names for each month:

January: Full Wolf Moon; Full Old Moon
February: Full Snow moon

March: Full Sap moon
April: Full Egg Moon
May: Full Milk Moon
June: Full Strawberry Moon
July: Full Thunder Moon
August: Full Green Corn Moon
September: Full Barley or Full Corn Moon
October: Full Harvest Moon
November: Full Beaver Moon
December: Full Long Nights Moon

The Old Julian calendar:

1. March 1, or 20-21 or 25 as the first month and New Year's Day.
2. April
3. May
4. June
5. July
6. August
7. September
8. October
9. November
10. December
11. January
12. February

Note: the Old Julian calendar is 13 days behind the Gregorian calendar today up to 2100 A.D. By 3001 A.D. it will be 21 days behind.

The Gregorian calendar:

1. January 1 is the first month and New Year's Day.

2. February
3. March
4. April
5. May
6. June
7. July
8. August
9. September
10. October
11. November
12. December

The polar opposite months:

January=July
February=August
March=September
April=October
May=November
June=December

Holidays:

January 1: New Year's Day Gregorian.
January 15: Martin King's Birthday.
January-February: Chinese New Year begins second new Moon after winter solstice.
February 14: Saint Valentine's Day.
February-March: Purim.
March 13: Saint Patrick's Day.
March-April: New Year's Day to the Bible.
March-April: Passover.
March-April: Easter.
May: Jesus ascension.

May: Mother's Day.
May: Memorial Day.
May-June: Pentecost and law given on mount Sinai.
June: Father's Day.
July 4: U.S. Independence Day.
September-October: Jewish New Year; Yom Kippur; feast of Tabernacles.
September: Labor Day-U.S.
October 12: Columbus Day.
October 31: Halloween, All Saints Eve.
November 1: All Saints Day; New Year's Day by ancient Anglo-Saxon.
November 2: Day of the dead.
November 11: Veterans Day and Old Halloween.
November's fourth Thursday: Thanksgiving in the U.S.
November-December: Chanukah.
December 24-25: Christmas Eve and Day.
December 31: New Year's Eve.

The Bible months:

1. March-April beginning on a new Moon
2. April-May
3. May-June
4. June-July
5. July-August
6. August-September
7. September-October
8. October-November
9. November-December
10. December-January
11. January-February
12. February-March

Note: These are of course our Gregorian months to the numbers of that of the Bible months, which are lunar starting on around a new Moon. Because of time differences and the Jewish people starting their new Moon not on the conjunction as we do the start of their months may start a day or to different. For example, September 25, 2003 is the new Moon UT, but the Jewish people started their New Year at sunset on September 26. Due to this sometimes the 24th day can mean the 26th day and the 26th day can be the 24th. You also can translate coded dates as a mixture between our calendars and theirs. If the first month and 24th day is mentioned you can translate it as September 26 even if the lunar calendar is different in that year and isn't actually the 24th day of that month according to the lunar calendar. Using a lunar calendar changes the dates of the Jewish faith each year, such as, Passover, Pentecost, Rosh Hashanah, Yom Kippur, the feast of Tabernacles and so on.

The Jewish Civil calendar:

1. September-October
2. October-November
3. November-December
4. December-January
5. January-February
6. February-March
7. March-April
8. April-May
9. May-June
10. June-July
11. July-August
12. August-September

Note: The Jewish Civil calendar is also a lunar calendar.

The above is our months in numbers to theirs. Since the lunar calendar is about 10-11 days behind our solar calendar every three years they add an extra month. Note the New Year starting points on each calendar. You'll need to remember them to understand the code of dates in prophecy and philosophy. The Jewish Civil calendar starting in our September-October makes their year, which is different then our year, to be our next year in this code. For example, the Hebrew Civil year of September 23, 2006 is 5765, but would be our year 2007 starting then. Isaiah 42 being our year 1942 translated to the Jewish Civil year would start their New Year of our 1942 in September or October 1941. Making December 7, 1941 their year 1942 the same chapter number of our 1942 of Isaiah 42. The war of Isaiah 42 was that of WWII when Japan attacked Pearl Harbor then and we entered that war the next day. The fire around about in Isaiah 42 could be that of the Leo zone where Hawaii and Pearl Harbor are in and the fire of ships attack then. Leo is a fire sign.

Creation's calendar:

1.May-June
2.June-July
3.July-August
4.August-September
5.September-October
6.October-November
7.November-December
8.December-January
9.January-February
10. February-March
11. March-April
12. April-May

Note: The book of Peter tells us that creation started in the month that Noah's flood happen. Genesis claims that month as the second month to the Bible calendar of May. The book of Revelation claims Alpha and Omega or the beginning and end is that in June when that book was written down. The ancient Egyptian calendar started its New Year's Day near the summer solstice or in July. If Creation's calendar is translated to a lunar one the first month could be June into July also and the rest of the months numbered there after.

Ancient Egyptian calendar:

1. June-July
2. July-August
3. August-September
4. September-October
5. October-November
6. November-December
7. December-January
8. January-February
9. February-March
10. March-April
11. April-May
12. May-June

Note: One of the ancient Egyptian calendar started when the dog star Sirius appeared in the east near dawn near the summer solstice or late June or July. The Nile would soon flood shortly after, which they connected to a good harvest and a brand new start of the year (New Year's Day and first month).

The Chinese calendar:

1. January-February
2. February-March
3. March-April
4. April-May
5. May-June
6. June-July
7. July-August
8. August-September
9. September-October
10. October-November
11. November-December
12. December-January

Note: The Chinese New Year begins on the day of the second new Moon after the Winter solstice.

Moslem's Sabbath: Friday

Next pieces of knowledge to help us understand this code is that of time. Below are different times:

Old Testament: New Testament:

Morning until 10am Third hour 6am to 9am
Heat of the day until 2pm sixth hour 9am to 12 noon
Cool of the day until 6pm Ninth hour 12 to 3pm
First watch 6pm to midnight 12th hour 3pm to 6pm
Second watch midnight to 3am First watch 6pm to 9pm
Third watch 3am to 6am Second watch 9pm to 12 am
Third watch 12am to 3am
Fourth watch 3am to 6am

The Jewish start to the day: The U.S. start of the day:

Sunset to sunset Midnight to midnight

Creation's start of the day:

Sunset to sunset until rotation was reverse and it made it from sunrise to sunrise.

Note: One other start of the day is sunrise to sunrise as the gospels tell of the ninth hour being that of about 3pm, which means the start is about 6am or about sunrise. One parable also states that the 11-12 hour is about evening making the start again about 6am or around sunrise.

God the Father: God the Son: God the Holy Ghost:

Sunrise 12 noon Sunset

Satan:

12 midnight (See Luke 22:53).

Military time:

00:00-00:59=12 midnight to 12:59am
01:00-01:59=1am to 1:59am
02:00-02:59=2am to 2:59am
03:00-03:59=3am to 3:59am
04:00-04:59=4am to 4:59am
05:00-05:59=5am to 5:59am
06:00-06:59=6am to 6:59am
07:00-07:59=7am to 7:59am
08:00-08:59=8am to 8:59am

09:00-09:59=9am to 9:59am
10:00-10:59=10am to 10:59am
11:00-11:59=11am to 11:59am
12:00-12:59=12pm to 12:59pm
13:00-13:59=1pm to 1:59pm
14:00-14:59=2pm to 2:59pm
15:00-15:59=3pm to 3:59pm
16:00-16:59=4pm to 4:59pm
17:00-17:59=5pm to 5:59pm
18:00-18:59=6pm to 6:59pm
19:00-19:59=7pm to 7:59pm
20:00-20:59=8pm to 8:59pm
21:00-21:59=9pm to 9:59pm
22:00-22:59=10pm to 10:59pm
23:00-23:59=11pm to 11:59pm

Note: The time zones on some world maps shows not only the time zones, but the longitude and latitude which plays an important part in my code. It also should be noted that UT (Universal time) is five hours later then Eastern U.S. time. Many astronomical times are UT times. So don't get confused. A solar or lunar eclipse UT can be a day earlier U.S. time. And also remember the international date line when traveling West from the U.S. goes from our day to the next day when crossed. A Sunday here becomes Monday there when you cross that line.

Below are what letters of different alphabets have become to be known as:

A=ox
B=house
C=camel
D=fish or door

E=he
I=arm
K=hand
M=water
N=snake-fish
O=eye
R=head
S=bow or tooth
T=mark

Below are the numbers to the English alphabet:

1. A
2. B
3. C
4. D
5. E
6. F
7. G
8. H
9. I
10. J
11. K
12. L
13. M
14. N
15. O
16. P
17. Q
18. R
19. S
20. T
21. U
22. V

23. W
24. X
25. Y
26. Z

Below is Chinese astrology that plays into my code:

Dog:1982
Pig:1983
Rat:1984
Ox:1985
Tiger:1986
Rabbit:1987
Dragon:1988
Snake:1989
Horse:1990
Sheep:1991
Monkey:1992
Rooster:1993
Dog:1994
Pig:1995
Rat:1996
Ox:1997
Tiger:1998
Rabbit:1999
Dragon:2000
Snake:2001
Horse:2002
Sheep:2003
Monkey:2004
Rooster:2005
Dog:2006
Pig:2007
Rat:2008

Ox:2009
Tiger:2010
Rabbit:2011
Dragon:2012
Snake:2013
Horse:2014
Sheep:2015
Monkey:2016
Rooster:2017
Dog:2018
Pig:2019

Note: Not all years are mentioned. I put in the years that are important in prophecy. If other years are of importance to you just subtract or add 12 years to the years from your year to one of the years above to see what sign you or they are. When going from A.D. to B.C. do not count the year zero.

1.Rat=11pm-1am; December; Sagittarius; opposite Horse; compatible with the Dragon and Monkey. Yang, water.
2.Ox=1am-3am; January; Capricorn; opposite sheep; compatible with the Snake and Rooster. Yin, water.
3.Tiger=3am-5am; February; Aquarius; opposite Monkey; compatible with the Horse and Dog. Yang, wood.
4.Rabbit=5am-7am; March; Pisces; opposite Rooster; compatible with the Sheep and Pig. Yin, wood.
5.Dragon=7am-9am; April; Aries; opposite Dog; compatible with the Monkey and Rat. Yang, wood.
6.Snake=9am-11am; May; Taurus; opposite Pig; compatible with the Rooster and Ox. Yin, fire.
7.Horse=11am-1pm; June; Gemini; opposite Rat; compatible with the Tiger and Dog. Yang, fire.

8.Sheep=1pm-3pm; July; Cancer; opposite Ox; compatible with the Pig and Rabbit. Yin, fire.

9.Monkey=3pm-5pm; August; Leo; opposite Tiger; compatible with the Dragon and Rat. Yang, metal.

10.Rooster=5pm-7pm; September; Virgo; opposite Rabbit; compatible with the Snake and Ox. Yin, metal.

11.Dog=7pm-9pm; October; Libra; opposite Dragon; compatible with the Horse and Tiger. Yin, metal.

12.Pig=9pm-11pm; November; Scorpio; opposite Snake; compatible with the Rabbit and Sheep. Yin, water.

Yin=female, cool, wet, passive, night, negative, left, north, winter, water, empty, Moon, death.

Yang=male, hot, dry, active, day, positive, right, south, summer, fire, full, life, Sun.

Note: The Chinese Rooster could be what the ancient Egyptians consider as the duck in their writings and carvings. The Chinese Dog is that of the ancient Egyptian jackal. The Chinese Ox could be the bull. The Chinese Tiger could be the lion. The Chinese Monkey is that of the Baboon, as well as other monkeys. Remember that Chinese astrology is that of years and hours instead of our astrology of months. And you can compare prophecies with this Chinese astrology as to our signs and months and places along with their polar opposites. For example, the Rooster can be our month of September and our Virgo sign. The Rat can be our month of December and the Sagittarius sign and opposite June and Gemini sign. When you come to a Chinese sign you can always look at its polar opposite for the true meaning sometimes of Chinese astrology and our astrology, as well as, both combined together. Polar opposites are the same signs in astrology, no matter what astrology you use. The same with our months and days.

A man wrote a book about how Psalm 1-100 were after the years of this 20th century. I took this and went one step further (or should I say many steps forward) by relating other books to this same idea. John Hogue is also doing this in quatrain numbers of Nostradamus century writings. What I did is to connect Isaiah, Ezekiel, Daniel, Micah, and Revelation as having certain years as their meaning of chapter numbers. Remember you also can take that year and add on to it with numbers or symbols of numbers given in each chapter in question. So don't say Isaiah 21 has no meaning for when you add 70 years to it and then see the meaning as the year 1991 when the first Iraq war started as Isaiah chapter 21 predicted. Or we can say Psalm 74 has no meaning to 1974, but when we add 21 years to it we get April of 1995 (the Oklahoma City bombing).

I learned awhile back how certain chapter numbers in the Bible equals certain years today. Since that time I have learned additional chapter or verse numbers to our years. You also could apply this same theory to Nostradamus' quatrains and other books.

Here's a list of what one author believed was Psalm chapters 1-101 are equal to our years and what I believed are other chapter numbers and verse numbers relating to our years:

Genesis 1-50=1954-2003
Deuteronomy 1-34=1976-2009
Job 1-42=1966-2007
Psalm 1-150=1901-2050
Proverbs 1-31=1976-2006
Ecclesiastes 1-12=2001-2012

Song of Solomon 1-8=2001-2008
Isaiah 1-66=1901-1966.
Jeremiah 1-52=1955-2006
Lamentations 1-5=2004-2008
Ezekiel 1-48=1901-1948.
Daniel 1-12=1989-2000.
Hosea 1-14=2000-2013
Joel 1-3=2004-2006
Amos 1-9=1995-2003
Micah 1-7=1995-2001.
Obadiah verses 1-21=1997-2017
Habakkuk 1-3=1995-1997
Zephaniah 1-3=2001-2003
Haggai 1-2=2004-2005
Zechariah 1-14=1994-2007
Malachi 1-4=2006-2009
Matthew 1-28=1981-2008
Mark 1-16=1989-2004
Luke 1-24=1981-2004
John 1-21=1986-2006
Acts 1-28=1976-2003
II Peter 1-3=2004-2006
Jude verses 1-28=2001-2033
Revelation 1-22=1981-2002

Note: There may be years to chapter numbers of other books in the Bible not listed above, but I am unaware of them at this time. Also remember that verse numbers can mean weeks, days, years, months, signs, age, even hours, minutes, longitude, latitude, along with symbolism of astrology and numerology. For example, Mathew 24:48-51 verses can mean ages 48-51 years old and chapter 24 reversed and doubled is 84 years old. The hand can mean the date of 27 because each hand has 27 bones in it. It can also mean Monday as the Moon or Cancer sign, which is given the numbers 2-7 or 27. Everything has a deep and hidden meaning. Nothing is vague or meaningless. As you read this book you will see that.

The other steps I went forward on in this concept is that chapter verses along with the chapter numbers can mean the year/month/week/day/hour/minute. The ancient prophecies often mention changing years to days or days to years and I went in more details to add these others. Ezekiel 4:6 tells us to change days to years. Important years, days, weeks and months are 3-4, 11-12, 21, 50 (Jubilee), 52 (Mayan calendar; deck of cards; weeks in our years),70, 430, 360, 2520, 1260, 1290, 1335, 2300. I also reverse the numbers and add and/or subtract the number of verses or chapter numbers as whole or in part to calculate to the correct date given. All of this is basically simple mathematics a child could do and may seem at first silly weak and stretched out. There's an old saying of in weakness there is strength and that a little child shall lead them. Both could mean a simple formula of mathematics, Chinese astrology or our astrology, numerology and these simple concepts and translations methods I used, a child could figure out yet not one has to this point. And what they show us are some of the most detailed accurate ancient prophecies of all time. Below are the calculations of time periods in this code I use:

1.One day=year=thousand years/24 hours=41.6 years as one hour.
2.One week=seven yearsx360=1260 days or years minus 18-19 days or years=1241-1242 days or years.
3.One month=29 and a half days to a lunar calendar
4.One year=360 days to God or 365.24 days to the Gregorian Calendar.
5.The 1260 days=years=1260x5.24=6602.4 days divided

by 360=18.34 minus 1260 days or years=1241.66 days or years.

6.The 1290 days=years=1290x5.24=6759.6 divided by 360=18.77 minus 1290 day or years=1271.22 days or years.

7.The 1335 days=years=1335x5.24=6995.4 divided by 360=19.43 minus 1335 days or years=1315.56 days or years.

8.The 3.5 years or time, times and half or 42 months is 1260 days or the number of days or years subtracting the 5.24 extra day years.

9.The 21 days=years=210 years or 12 years or 12 weeks reversed.

10.From night to morning=11-12 hours=years

11.From morning to evening=11-12 hours=years

12.The 42 months=1260 days or years or the number mentioned above after subtracting the 5.25 extra days a year.

13. The 3 weeks=21 days/years/210 years

14. Three weeks=three years

15. The 2520 years or days after seven years it took Solomon to build the temple of God in Jerusalem.

16.The 70 years of Jeremiah captivity of the Jews and Jerusalem laid waste.

Note: These calculations are approximate because 5.24 maybe more exact like 5.2457 or some other close number that does make a difference. This is because our year is not exactly 365.24 days. God's year for some reason is 360 days long instead of our year of 365.24 days. Sometime when days are given and changed to years you multiply that number of years by 5.24 days and then divide by 360 and subtract from the final number. For example, 1260 days equals 1260 years times 5.24 days equals 6602.4 divided by

360 equals 18.34 minus 1260 days=1241.66. You also can deduct 5.24 days from every year of ours. Ezekiel 4:6 tells us to change day for year or vice versa. You also can add the original number of days and subtract 18-19 days from the end of it even though you counted out the exact number of days. When you do this you change the days to years then back to days. For example, November 18-19, 2004 is 1335 days from March 25, 2001. Subtract 18-19 days from that and you come to October 31 and November 1, 2004.

You also can add zeros to a number or between a number. For example, 27 can have two zeros added in between to make 20:07 military time of 8:07 p.m. You also can add zeros to the end of a set number. Take Daniel's chapter 10 twenty one days. Add a zero to the end of 21 and you have 210 days or years subtracted from 542 B.C. and it equals 332 B.C. the date or close to when Alexander the great came and conquered Babylon which Daniel 10:20 predicted.

Sometime the atomic chart numbers are important to some prophecies and knowledge. Below are some of those numbers of the elements:

1-Hydrogen;2-Helium;3-Lithium;4-Beryllium;5-Baron;6-Carbon;7-   Nitrogen;8-Oxygen;9-Fluorine;10-Neon;11-Sodium;12-Magnesium;13-   Aluminum;14-Silicon;15-Phosphorus;16-Sulfur;...and so on. For all of them look at the atomic element chart in a science book.

Note: Each number equals the numbers of proton, electron and neutrons to each atom. Lithium for example would have three electrons, three neutrons and three protons. The Father, Son and Holy Ghost are symbols of 1-2-3; or 14-15-16: as Hydrogen, Helium and Lithium; and Silicon, Phosphorus and Sulfur. Lithium would be that of 999 as there are three electrons, three neutrons and three protons making 9 or 3x9=27 or three nines=999. Silicon would be the Father of computer chips made out of that atom. Sand or silicon is what computer chips are made out of as Ezekiel 28 claimed 2500 B.C. And Jesus as the Son is Phosphorus as is connected to Venus in Greek dictionary. And the Holy Ghost is Sulfur as is connected to fire that symbolizes the presence of the Holy Ghost and baptism in fire and tongues of fire as the books of Ezekiel 28, Acts and as the New Testament tells us. Samson's great power was in his hair. Atomic element 16 is sulfur, which makes up hair and is the power and strength of the trinity of God as the Holy Ghost. The Holy Ghost is also the wind as told in the Book of Acts. The air signs of Gemini (when Pentecost happen 30 A.D. with the rushing of a mighty wind), Libra and Aquarius are all air or wind signs. Birds are also the symbol of wind or air signs are what govern all things as Ecclesiastes 10:20 claims. Does that mean the same thing science is now telling us that all things are govern by another. The butterfly effect they call it. A butterfly fluttering its wings in China can cause a hurricane to form in the Atlantic. Was this what Jesus meant by a sparrow doesn't fall to the ground without his Father (Holy Ghost) knowing it? And that is what Ecclesiastes 10:20 means when a bird shall tell (predict) the matter and tell of extreme knowledge? It wasn't some cute little saying, but actually giving the details of modern science!!!

Below is the listings in numbers of the books of the Old and New Testament:

Old Testament:
1. Genesis
2. Exodus
3. Leviticus
4. Numbers
5. Deuteronomy

6. Joshua
7. Judges
8. Ruth
9. I Samuel
10. II Samuel
11. I Kings
12. II Kings
13. I Chronicles
14. II Chronicles
15. Ezra
16. Nehemiah
17. Esther
18. Job
19. Pslams
20. Proverbs
21. Ecclesiastes
22. The Song of Solomon
23. Isaiah
24. Jeremiah
25. Lamentations
26. Ezekiel
<u>27. Daniel</u>
28. Hosea
29. Joel
30. Amos
31. Obadiah
32. Jonah
33. Micah
34. Nahum
35. Habakkuk
36. Zephaniah
37. Haggai
38. Zechariah
39. Malachi

Books of the New Testament:

1. Matthew
2. Mark
3. Luke
4. John
5. Acts
6. Romans
7. I Corinthians
8. II Corinthians
9.Galatians
10. Ephesians
11. Philippians
12. Colossians
13. I Thessalonians
14. II Thessalonians
15. I Timothy
16. II Timothy
17. Titus
18. Philemon
19. Hebrews
20. James
21. I Peter
22. II Peter
23. I John
24. II John
25. III John
26. Jude
27. Revelation

Remember these book numbers because sometimes they come into play with the coded prophecies. Psalms, for example, is the 19th book symbolic of September 19 and the

19 before the years 01-99 of Psalms 1-99. The books of Daniel and Revelation are both the 27ᵗʰ book from the Old and New Testaments. A date, or day (Monday), when September 27, 2003 was as an important in future prophecies.

When I say Hebrew or Greek word or words and give numbers in this book I mean those numbers in the Hebrew and Greek dictionaries of the *Strong's concordance of the Bible* with the Greek and Hebrew dictionaries. Sometime words near those words in those dictionaries also have meaning to what you are looking up.

About the Author:

Kurt Brian Bakley was born 8:11 p.m. Friday evening October 15, 1954 at Cooper Hospital in Camden, New Jersey across the river from Philadelphia during Hurricane Hazel. He grew up hating books, reading and writing because of his eye problems and learning disabilities and dropped out of high school. Then one Saturday night when he was 21 years old, after partying that night, he woke up early Sunday morning with massive amount of knowledge and yearning to read, write and research all kinds of knowledge. He went out first thing that Sunday morning to the mall and waited till noon for the bookstore to open. He immediately went in and bought several books and began his reading, writing and researching to this day. That was on August 29 of 1976 and today (2011) he is still reading, writing and researching information on prophecy and Christianity. He has over 50,000 hours of research and writing from then to now (2011), his 35th year of doing so. This is his eighth book from 2008 that he's written. Those eight books are: *The Nativity*; *The Antichrist*; *The Experiment in Philadelphia: Did Einstein discover God?*; *The boy who could predict earthquakes*; *2012: The two earthquakes and God's two witnesses*; *Prophecies that have, will, or didn't happen*; *The balanced life*; and the eighth is *The Life of Kurt B. Bakley* available now (September 2011). All eight books are available at this web site: WWW. authorhouse.Com. now (September of 2011). Read them in this order, first, *The Nativity*, then *The Antichrist*, then the next, *The Experiment at Philadelphia*, then *The boy who could predict earthquakes,* then *2012: The two earthquakes and God's two witnesses,* then the *Prophecies that have, will, or didn't happen,* then *The balanced life* and then *The Life of Kurt B. Bakley.* After you read them once read them through the second time slowly and then start to read his the ninth book *Predictions of 2013-2014*, then the *Predictions for 2015*, and then *Predictions for 2019*, and then *Predictions for 2016-2018*, available in the future at the web site above. When you read them in that order read them from cover to cover, start with the rear cover then the introduction and all the way through. Do not skip round or you will get confused. Don't stop because you have a question or don't understand or want to look up documentation. They are all a hard read but bare with them. You can look up documentation on the second round through when you read them for the second time. After that second round read through start reading my other books in this order: *The Mayan Code, The mystery of God, The mystery of good and evil, The Divine Code, The Divine Code 2, The Divine Code 3*. Remember in the two books *The mystery of God* and *The Mystery of good and evil* are both written from the antichrist's view. Read these last six books after you read twice or more the 12 mentioned above. Revelation chapter 5 predicts these books are the seven eyes and seven horns that go around the world on the World Wide Web (WWW). The last six are to be the last six books of mine you are read to make 18 books (12+6=18). Is the satellite that powers the world wide web ten by 20 cubits as Zechariah 5:1-2 predicted for a great flying (satellite) roll (a round satellite-ancient book) that size? On the web site: WWW. Authorhouse.com just type in my name Kurt B. Bakley in the search box and then click the go or search and all or most of my books will come up. Type Kurt Bakley for my other books. *The Divine Code* published in April of 2001 predicts planes flying into buildings in New York City on September 16-17, 2001. Five or six days off but still an amazing prophecy. That same book predicted the new millenium to start June 21, 2001. Nothing happened then, but the Bible's ancient prophecies documented in that book is that date. My book *Prophecies that have, will, and didn't happen* show that certain ancient Bible prophecies are detailed and correct, but fail to happen. My book *The Divine Code 2* documented how the Bible predicted a vile person to come to power in Russia born in the Taurus sign and start a war and invade the Middle East, Israel and Florida. Such a person ran for President of Russia in 1996 born in the Taurus sign and promised to invade the Middle East, but he failed to be elected. The book *The Divine Code 2* shows prophecies of TWA flight 800 explosion and crash off of Long Island near a place called Babylon. It tells of ancient prophecies that gives the place and attitude and what caused it to explode. *The Divine Code 3* tells of ancient prophecies for certain years that didn't come true, but may in the future in 2017-2018. *The Mayan Code* predicts the exact date of the end of the world using ancient prophecies of the Mayan and the Bible. *The mystery of God* shows how science, physics and the Philadelphia experiment answers all questions that people had about the Bible and all things. It is written from the antichrist's view point. *The mystery of good and evil* explains creation and how it happen and how all things work in the Universe. Again it is written in the antichrist's view point. *The Mayan Code*, *The mystery of good and evil* and *The Divine Code 3* may no longer be available. Look at the copyright page of each of my books to see when they were published so you can't say they were written after the fact. Do what ever the angel tells you. If the Authorhouse web site changes call 1-888-519-5121 and ask them for the new web site or order all these books above by phone at that number and extension 5022. If you can't find them type in the title of the book. Keep trying till you get through by either internet or by phone. The web site and phone lines may be jam for all the orders and it may take several hours or days or weeks or months to get through. Remember what the angel tells you the one time it appears or the two times it appears to you.